Bodies of Water

Lakes and Ponds

Cassie Mayer

Heinemann
LIBRARY

www.heinemann.co.uk/library
Visit our website to find out more information about Heinemann Library books.

To order:
 Phone 44 (0) 1865 888066
Send a fax to 44 (0) 1865 314091
 Visit the Heinemann Bookshop at www.heinemann.co.uk/library to browse our
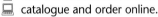 catalogue and order online.

First published in Great Britain by Heinemann Library, Halley Court, Jordan Hill, Oxford OX2 8EJ, part of Harcourt Education. Heinemann is a registered trademark of Harcourt Education Ltd.

Editorial: Diyan Leake and Cassie Mayer
Design: Joanna Hinton-Malivoire
Picture research: Erica Martin
Production: Duncan Gilbert

Originated by Chroma Graphics (Overseas) Pte Ltd
Printed and bound in China by South China Printing Co. Ltd

ISBN 978 0 4311 8472 2

11 10 09 08 07
10 9 8 7 6 5 4 3 2 1

British Library Cataloguing in Publication Data
Mayer, Cassie
Bodies of Water: Lakes

A full catalogue record for this book is available from the British Library

Acknowledgements
The publishers would like to thank the following for permission to reproduce photographs: Alamy pp. **11** (Brian Atkinson), **13** (Alfa Foto Agency), **19** (Che Garman), **20** (Pixonnet. com), **21** (BL Images Ltd), **23** (shallow pond: Brian Atkinson; freight ship: Pixonnet.com); Corbis pp. **4** (NASA), **8** (Theo Allofs), **10** (Bob Krist), **18** (Tom Grill); Getty Images pp. **6** (National Geographic/Michael S. Lewis), **7** (Stone/Russell Kaye/Sandra-Lee Phipps), **9** (LOOK/Florian Werner), **14** (Lonely Planet/Mark Newman), **15** (Digital Vision), **16** (National Geographic/George Grall), **17** (John Bracegirdle), **23** (lake in a valley: Digital Vision), **back cover** (LOOK/Florian Werner); Jupiter Images p. **5** (Brand X Pictures/Don Mason).

Cover photograph of Lake Yamdrok-Tso, Tibet reproduced with permission of Corbis/Zefa (Serge Kozak).

Every effort has been made to contact copyright holders of any material reproduced in this book. Any omissions will be rectified in subsequent printings if notice is given to the publishers.

Contents

Lakes

water

Most of the Earth is covered by water.

Some of this water is in lakes.

A lake is a large area covered by water.

Most lakes have fresh water.
The water is not salty.

Lakes have land on all sides.

Lakes are smaller than oceans.

Ponds

pond

A pond is a very small lake.

Ponds are shallow.

How lakes form

higher land

lake

higher land

Lakes form in low areas of the land.
The land around the lake is higher.

The low land fills with water.
The low land becomes a lake.

Some lakes are near mountains.

valley

Some lakes are in valleys.

Lake life

turtle

Lakes can have many animals.
People like to fish in lakes.

Lakes can have many plants.
The tall plants are called reeds.

How we use lakes

The water in lakes is cleaned.
Then people can drink the water.

People use pipes to bring lake water to them.

Some lakes are so big that huge ships can sail on them.

People like to take boat rides
on lakes.

Lake facts

Lake Baikal is the largest lake in the world. It is in Russia.

Lake Superior is the second largest lake in the world. It is in the United States and Canada.

Picture glossary

goods things that people buy and sell

shallow does not go down far; not deep

valley a low area of land. Valleys are between mountains or hills.

Index

Notes for parents and teachers

Before reading

Ask the children if they know the difference between a lake and a pond. Explain that lakes are very large and deep. They are very important because they contain the water that we need for our homes. Many important animals live in lakes.

After reading

Little lakes. Take the children out to look at a puddle or make a puddle. Ask them to tell you what they can see in the puddle. Is the water smooth or does it move? Explain that puddles are like very tiny lakes.

Lake game. Teach the children the traditional rhyme: "As I was walking round the lake, I met a little rattle snake. I gave him so much jelly cake, it made his little belly ache. One, two three: Out goes he/she (as appropriate)." The children stand in a circle and one child stands in the middle, eyes shut, while the others chant the rhyme. When the group finishes chanting, the child points at a person and that person has to sit down.

Water talk. Talk to the children about how water is taken from the lakes, goes through a cleaning process, and then is piped to our homes and schools. Ask them what things they can think of that needs water. Make a list and display this on the wall. Add to the list during the day.